28 Habitudes and Attitudes of Successful Small Business Entrepreneurs

Peter K. Black

Copyright © 2014 Pierre Jereczek

All rights reserved

To my readers and my wonderfull wife

Table of Contents

We all have the capacity to do great things; there are those who are born winners but those who are self-made got to have an even greater adventure.

I think. Therefore I am.

We are what we repeatedly do.

Excellence therefore is not an act but a habit.

Getting on the road to success.

Tip #1: Be passionate about your work.

Tip #2: Greet the sunrise every day.

Tip #3: Have a daily goal and accomplish it every day.

Tip #4: Learn to relax and be productive at the same time.

Tip #5: Put great value in people and relationships.

Tip #6: Lead by example.

Tip #7: Challenge your 'team' to be the best they can be in any situation.

Tip #8: Know how and when to let go.

Tip #9: Do not be a profit-oriented.

Tip #10: Be vision-oriented instead of mistake-oriented.

Tip #11: Strive to accumulate skills not degrees.

Tip #12: Do not sweat the small stuff.

Tip #13: Even if you do not have time, try to 'make' time for everything.

Tip #14: Do not live other people's dreams.

Tip #15: Remember to think outside the box.

Tip #16: Be a risk-taker.

Tip #17: They believe that in order to discover new things, you must do things you have never done before.

Tip #18: Surround yourself with competent and talented people.

Tip #19: Learn how make plans but also know how to improvise.

Tip #20: Never be complacent.

Tip #21: Be confident and know how to handle criticism.

Tip #22: Never let a single dollar stay in your wallet.

Tip #23: Never forget to give yourself a salary, and pay yourself well.

Tip #24: Consider all opportunities, and do not weigh them in monetary value.

Tip #25: Learn to make do with whatever resources you've got.

Tip #26: They create the market by creating a need.

Tip #27: They do not spread themselves too thin.

Tip #28: Invest on things that grow more and more valuable in time.

WE ALL HAVE THE CAPACITY TO DO GREAT THINGS; THERE ARE THOSE WHO ARE BORN WINNERS BUT THOSE WHO ARE SELF-MADE GOT TO HAVE AN EVEN GREATER ADVENTURE.

Success is not exclusive to those who are born into a business empire. There are more success stories that have humble beginnings and more interestingly these entrepreneurs have more in common than you'd think. This is what this little book is all about - a compilation of habits and attitudes that make up a winner. Consider this a guide of sorts that can help you reach your goals and your entrepreneurial dreams.

Now, the mere fact that you picked up this book means you are on your way to success. Your eagerness to learn and broaden your knowledge is an attitude that will help you succeed. And the fact that you chose to be an entrepreneur means you have the audacity to succeed. But before we move on to the heart of the matter, let us first consider the two most important terminologies – attitude and habit.

I THINK. THEREFORE I AM.

Attitude is a state of mind or a feeling – a person's disposition. How we see our world and our situation is driven by our own state of mind. If you wish to succeed, we should have a positive winning attitude, no matter what the situation.

Now remember, our attitude is just a reflection of our state of mind, our opinions and our perceptions. If you feel that you are moving in circles in terms of your business, and you feel that you are failing, maybe it's time for an attitude change. Changing your outlook may just be the key to turning things around.

Success is man's battle against himself, to leave his comfort zone in order to follow unchartered paths. If you refuse to take risks and try something new, then the entrepreneur's arena might not be for you.

WE ARE WHAT WE REPEATEDLY DO. EXCELLENCE THEREFORE IS NOT AN ACT BUT A HABIT.

Aristotle knows precisely what he is talking about. Consider it this way, if you constantly apply yourself to doing things that would lead you to success, then you are in the habit of being successful.

But what exactly does habit mean? According to the dictionary, it is a recurrent, often conscious pattern of behavior that is acquired through frequent repetition. It is also synonymous to attitude as the second description is that habit is also and established disposition of the mind or character.

The good news is that we can change the way we think and we can teach ourselves to learn good habits.

Maxwell Marks sad in his book Psycho cybernetics that people develop a habit in just 21 days, while a study published in 2009 states that it takes a minimum of 66 days. But it does not matter how long it takes, the point is that we can form a habit, it is within our capacity to develop habits that lead to success.

GETTING ON THE ROAD TO SUCCESS.

Successful people have a lot of similarities but in this equation, we do not include circumstance and social status, we speak of parallels in the way they think and act. Because it is in these habits and character that we find the keys to success, in whatever field, whether it is parenthood or building a business empire.

The list you will find is not written in chronological way, nor is it written by manner of importance so you can start with number 5 or number 10 just for fun.

Tip #1: Be passionate about your work.

Entrepreneurs start a business because they are passionate about something, it may be a craft and idea or an advocacy. Then they build the business around this passion and that level enthusiasm is reflected in everything they produce and in the kind of service that they offer. Have you ever been in a store where even the entrance is welcoming and the somehow even without the coaxing of that staff, you would not want to leave without buying anything something from the store? This passion in action. When you love what you do, you never have to work a day in your life. You've probably heard that phrase a hundred times before but it is true. And if you do not feel like what you're doing is 'work' your level of commitment is off the charts, you don't care if you have been working for hours. You simply do not quit until you achieve what you perceive is perfection. What customers do not see, the hard work, long hours, moments of frustrations and joy, is hidden behind the effortless look and feel of the product or the exquisite flavor of the food.

Tip #2: Greet the sunrise every day.

Imagine a child waking up on Christmas day, there is urgency and excitement. This is probably why people who are driven to win wake up early. They are excited about the happenings of the day and they just could not wait to begin. If you often find that you drag yourself out of bed, dreading whatever awaits you that day then there is something wrong. You either change your sleeping pattern or you might just need a career change.

For the entrepreneur, the early hours are very crucial to planning the rest of the day. A renewed and rested mind functions better and you are sure that your decisions are not hurried or forced. It is also the best time of the day to reflect on what has transpired the previous day and learn from it – today is the best day to implement everything that is considered.

If you start your day, when everything starts to become hectic, you'll always feel that that there is never enough time to accomplish things and you end up staying in your office late when you should be having dinner with your family or friends.

Tip #3: Have a daily goal and accomplish it every day.

Goal setting is a practice that entrepreneurs love doing. They love measuring their progress and what better way to check on ones' accomplishments than doing it on a daily basis. An entrepreneur's calendar is always full and not because of non-stop meeting or conference. It's the 'to do' list that takes up most of the pages. And I would not be surprised if their lists are categorized.

In a way, this is how entrepreneurs challenge themselves to be more productive. This helps them ensure that they do not stray from their objective and to keep themselves focused. And a day without their calendar would be like leaving home naked, and a day without written goals is similar to walking around in a dark room.

Making a habit of taking regular self-assessment keeps you motivated and focused. It also helps you make decision making much easier. Deciding what to do next is easier when you know exactly where you are.

Tip #4: Learn to relax and be productive at the same time.

Entrepreneurs know that the most important non-renewable resource that they have is time. So they make it a point to make use of their time in the most productive way. And yes, knowing how and when to relax and recharge is also one of the skills that entrepreneurs have.

So, how do they relax and be productive at the same time? Here is an example, 'retail therapy' has a different meaning to successful entrepreneurs. While others do it for the pure joy of self-gratification, entrepreneurs get more out of it. For one, they take note of the store's visual merchandising and how effective it is. They look at the current trends and how it applies to their business. They are also on the lookout for new business opportunities and sometimes, they may be on the hunt for possible new members of their company.

When on a vacation or a weekend get-away, it is no different, they go to a new place and sight-see the business aspect of the operations. You would probably find them looking for possible new suppliers or talking to the managers about how many people they cater to and how many of those responded because of certain promotions.

Tip #5: Put Great Value in People and Relationships.

Successful entrepreneurs make sure that the people they regularly do business with are satisfied. Every single day, they deal with their staff, clients and suppliers. On top of this tier is staff morale, happy employees are more productive and they are more likely to have excellent output, whether it is service or product. Small business entrepreneurs regularly check on their employees and the daily operation. They do a lot of hands on supervision and quality check and they take this time to encourage camaraderie within the group. They also watch out for the personalities that may cause trouble. In a sea of positive energy, it's easy to spot negativity. Successful entrepreneurs know how to encourage and but exercise your authority at the same time. A warning to those who might have the tendency to be over-eager to please: too much familiarity is not a good thing either. You should be open, approachable but firm.

Your customers are your businesses' lifeblood. The simplest way to satisfy each one is to make sure that you deliver what you promise for the value you receive. Be honest in your dealings and make sure if anything goes wrong, you have a contingency plan. It is in these challenges that entrepreneurs thrive. They find satisfaction in finding solutions and are able to help other people in the process.

Entrepreneurs also aim for a long term relationship with their suppliers. First, they make sure that their suppliers reflect the same vision that they have. They also make sure that their suppliers are paid well and on time. This is true especially for those who are in the retail business. They even visit factories and help their suppliers find ways to improve production processes for the welfare of the factory workers and their families.

Trust, honesty and a heart for service are important in all of these relationships and these are traits that the entrepreneur should have if he is aims to succeed.

Tip #6: Lead by Example.

They don't just make the rules; they are the first to follow it diligently. People, no matter what age are prone to emulate their superiors, just as a child imitates her mother's morning make up regimen and his father's carpentry skills, so do employees tend to be like their boss. Successful entrepreneurs have a competent team working for them because they understand the concept of transference. They value their image especially how they are perceived by the staff. They see every situation with a kind of clarity, they perceive the possible impact of every action and how it ripples down to the last person on the organizational hierarchy. Eventually, they end up with a group who are likeminded, creating a workspace that is efficient and productive. Entrepreneurs succeed when they run the company in a positive way and this is a reflection of who they are. There are business owners who hire supervisors to watch over managers and managers to watch over everybody else. They set up rules and regulations along with sanctions and rewards. Most entrepreneurs are reward oriented, making use of incentives and profit sharing schemes for work well done. Sanctions create workers that are motivated by fear while rewards promote workers that are motivated by the need to be better.

Tip #7: Challenge your 'team' to be the best they can be in any situation.

They do not spoon feed their employees with strict manuals and stern operating procedures. They believe that teamwork is the backbone of their business. With this in mind, they see employees as team players and each an integral part of a whole. Whether it is a staff of four or fifty, they form a community working towards a singular goal – that is to be good at what they do and profit from it. This is also why they tend to choose who they work with carefully. Most of the time, they hire based on disposition and potential rather than educational background. They believe that a good working environment start with a positive mindset. This is also why even during the most hectic of days they still pull through because everyone is there to help one another.

Entrepreneurs allow their 'team' to make decisions and learn to take responsibility for it. This attitude develops employees who are confident and capable, they do not second guess themselves. This way, entrepreneurs avoid the tendency to micromanage.

Entrepreneurs not only provide livelihood, they also empower their staff by giving them a chance to grow in knowledge and experience, guiding them along the way.

Tip #8: Know how and when to let go.

This habit applies to all aspects of the business operation. Concepts and ideas sometimes work and sometimes they don't. Successful entrepreneurs know when to abandon an idea, or a brand or even the whole operation. They know when to turn their back, sell and move on. There is no point in contemplating and mulling over what went wrong, there is not time for mourning loss because they are not prone to give sentimental value to anything in the business. They put value in their advocacies but not the business itself.

If they started the business because they love to bake, they can still bake to their hearts fill and be happy with a smaller operation rather than running and managing a bakery with a full crew. If their reason to start the company is to provide livelihood to a community, their focus will never be to build a business empire but to make sure that the community becomes stable and self-sufficient. Then they move on to the next, taking with them only the experience, the knowledge and the relationships that was built because of it, if their pockets are a bit fuller than when they started, then that is only a bonus side effect, never the main objective.

TIP #9: DO NOT BE A PROFIT-ORIENTED.

The question some of you would ask is, why even go into business if not to be financially well off? A business whose main goal is to profit will not flourish. We all go into business believing that someday we will live comfortable lives, taking occasional vacations and shopping sprees. But that is not always the case, if that is your motivation to succeed, then you'll burn out on your first year. The timeframe for any business' return of investment (ROI) is usually more than a year. And most of the business' growing pains happen on the first year. The profits earned during this time seldom compensate for the late nights and the busy days.

Successful entrepreneurs do not look to the spreadsheet to measure their success, they measure it by the number of satisfied customers they have served that day and the families they have the privilege to provide for every single day.

Tip #10: Be vision-oriented instead of mistake-oriented.

Whoever invented strategic planning and team building is probably experts in managing big business. If you've been in any business seminars or have attended business courses, you'll be encouraged to write your company's vision and mission and do key indicator exercises that seem too corporate for some. But for the entrepreneur, they plan according to what they feel is right, they seldom follow status quo because they do not lose sight of their vision. They may feel less motivated at times but they know what they want. They begin with the end in mind and they do not lose sight of it.

In their everyday dealings, they are not on the lookout for obstacles (they just happen and they deal with it accordingly with a positive outlook) or what is wrong with the system. They simply find ways to make things better and use past mistakes as lessons on what not to do. They strategize from a positive point of view, directly putting their strengths into play from the very start.

Tip #11: Strive to accumulate skills not degrees.

Entrepreneurs are more interested in applied knowledge rather than theories. They would rather find things out for themselves. While education is important, let's face it, we only retain the knowledge that really interests us. So they go out to the real world and indulge in getting experience. You will hear of successful entrepreneurs who apprentice for skilled artists and self-made businessmen even if they do not get any compensation.

There are a lot of principles and lessons in life that we cannot learn in a classroom, we need to experience these life lessons in order for us to really say that we have learned them. This is the kind of education that you cannot put a price on but its value is worth more than any knowledge you accumulate during four year course. Take for example, how to deal with a supplier who never delivers on time but he sells the best raw meat in town. Or how to minimize rejects in a production line. These things greatly impact your daily operations and eventually your profits for the month or for that particular project. These situations call for your skill to negotiate with a valued supplier and the intimate knowledge of your product, things that are not in any syllabus of any course in any school.

Tip #12: Do not sweat the small stuff.

There are good days and there are bad days, some days just fly by and there are days that you can't wait to end. These are the kind of reality that entrepreneurs know intimately. How do they just breeze through? Simple. By not paying too much attention to the unimportant details. There are business people who love micromanaging, they think that a close monitoring of every single process and every single person's progress is crucial to the smooth operation of their business. This is why they get distressed when something goes wrong and they start to panic. Entrepreneurs go straight to figuring out solutions in a calm manner, looking at the big picture rather than the tiniest details. This is the difference between a businessman and an entrepreneur; the latter follows his own rules and the other play by pre-established guidelines.

Tip #13: Even if you do not have time, try to 'make' time for everything.

Sure, they have deadlines and schedules to keep but they know how to delegate tasks to competent people so they can dictate their own schedules. They are the kind of people who do not stop until the job is done and they work more than 20 hours a day. They do not keep this kind of work hours because they are trying to beat a deadline but because they are excited to complete their work or they just get so immersed in their project that they do not have any sense of time. Despite this routine, they take time to be with their family and friends and even their staff. They need it because these people are their support team, their ever loyal fan club. They understand that they need to take care of themselves, the mental and physical health.

Tip #14: Do Not Live Other People's Dreams.

One of the most important traits of a successful entrepreneur is the fact that they know what they want. You can suggest an idea or explain trends but they end up following their own. This is what makes them succeed. They do not just go with the flow, no matter how you present it, explain it with charts and scientific facts but still the entrepreneur will stay on his chosen path and they always prove themselves right. Most entrepreneurs start with an idea, and that idea keeps them up at night until they decide to start the project or business. Most of them know nothing about accounting, management or even food science (for restaurateurs) so along the way, they meet people with expertise in things they know nothing about. The surprising thing is, they only get the knowledge that they need and move on with what they want.

If you want to succeed, never second guess yourself; follow your convictions and ideas, not someone else's.

Tip #15: Remember to think outside the box.

This trait is what makes them different and one of the reasons why they succeed. They see things differently. Basically they are the ones who got excited when they found out that their Dad is Santa and their Mom is the Tooth Fairy. They could not wait to grow up and find out what magical being they would turn out to be. They see the challenge in obstacles, the opportunity in discarded things, the value of people who go through hardships and so on. They all the colors of the spectrum and they dare to try them all. There will always be people who try and encapsulate an idea and try to sell it as is while entrepreneurs allow it to have a life of its own. Consider the furniture maker who found herself in a city saturated with other furniture makers whose expertise goes farther back. She dove into it head on and showed her craft but then she had more to offer, while the other shops only sold the furniture pieces, she was selling the whole look. She added home décor to her line of products - the lamps, boxes and wall décor. Entrepreneurs are often called innovators and trendsetters, if you want to be one, you should start seeing the world differently and unleash your creativity.

Tip #16: Be a risk-taker.

Some say that entrepreneurs are 'calculated' risk taker but not all the time. They contemplate and weigh the pros and cons, and when they do make a decision, they stick to it. But for decisions where there is no way to predict, measure or calculate the future or the outcome, they follow their instincts. It is also their instinct that tells them when it's not the time to introduce ideas, a product or an invention. You may wonder at times when you see entrepreneurs expanding and building when the economy is at a low. This is instinct, experience and research coming into play, they would say that they are simply preparing for economic progress that is about to come. To some, it does not make sense then we get it when their ideas become a big hit.

Tip #17: They believe that in order to discover new things, you must do things you have never done before.

They are not afraid to leave their comfort zone and explore the great beyond. The more they step forward, the bolder they become. More importantly, they do not regret the decisions they have made. Their philosophy is "how will you know what is out there if you do not "get out there"? How will you know if anything works if you don't even try"? It does not matter to them if and when they reach a dead end because there are no pointless journeys, the way back is a worthwhile adventure in itself.

Tip #18: Surround yourself with competent and talented people.

Entrepreneurs know the limits of their capacity and they know how to delegate the rest. If they do not know how something works, they get an expert to teach them. If they are not good in any aspect of the business, they are not afraid to consult or hire someone who knows. And oftentimes, they see the potential in certain people and they invest in that talent, they give their people enough room and resources to develop their skills.

Tip #19: Learn how make plans but also know how to improvise.

An entrepreneur's day is full of surprises, and they know this full well. This is why they make plans but leave room for change. They believe that the only thing constant in our world is change and adaptability is one of the first lessons they learn. Nothing is certain until the day ends but they never lose sight of the goal and by the time all is said in done, they make sure that they deliver, just as promised.

Tip #20: Never be complacent.

Even when the daily operations are running smoothly, they are ready for anything. They surely have a backup plan and a backup for the backup plan. Yes, it looks like a lot of work, intensive planning and critical thinking, but this where the entrepreneur thrives. They do not cease to be on top of the whole operation and they refuse to rest on their laurels. They understand that a business is a fragile thing, a small tip of the scale and everything can just go the other direction. They succeed because they find the balance between control and letting things just happen.

Tip #21: Be confident and know how to handle criticism.

You cannot please everybody; it's the side-effect of our diversity. Our differences are what make us beautiful and interesting. The entrepreneur's critics become their motivation and sometimes their reason to give a good hearty laugh. Besides, if you have critics following you that means they are paying attention, even if the feedback is a negative one. Entrepreneurs are not dissuaded by mere assumptions and opinions because they know exactly who they are, what they want and what direction they want to take.

Criticism, whether they are constructive or downright negative can be helpful too. If taken in a different perspective, it can help you improve or strengthen your business processes.

Tip #22: Never let a single dollar stay in your wallet.

Make sure it has somewhere to go - where it has the potential to comeback double or triple in value. Most entrepreneurs do not leave their hard earned cash to live a static and slow life in the bank, it is in constant motion. The life cycle of your money should be short and its regeneration should be on the upward positive side. Withdrawals and deposits happen every day because money should not be kept like a valued jewel in a vault, because money is simply a means to an end. Besides, money kept under lock and key depreciates, a jewel on the other hand appreciates. It's not that money does not have value, it does, but it is a resource that should be constantly used in order for it to grow. Remember that you do not work for money; you let it work for you. So you use it to build, create, market and sell two folds or threefold.

Tip #23: Never forget to give yourself a salary, and pay yourself well.

If you do not include your salary to your costs, then you are giving it for free. Your ideas and services have value and they are some of your greatest assets. If you do not take care of yourself, then who will? Startup entrepreneurs have a tendency to exclude their own salaries from their expenses and this is a big mistake. If money is tight, do not exclude your pay, just input the amount in the payables account and give your business enough time to pay you back. Remember that whatever you add is the business's' capital and the business owns it, not yours. Do not confuse your compensation with the business' capital funds.

TIP #24: CONSIDER ALL OPPORTUNITIES, AND DO NOT WEIGH THEM IN MONETARY VALUE.

Sometimes the experience is worth more than the money you will earn. Our education should always be coupled with experience, and then it becomes invaluable. The opportunities that come our way may never pass the same way again, so before you turn your back on opportunities that are presented to you, consider it, sleep on it and then decide.

Tip #25: Learn to make do with whatever resources you've got.

This is the entrepreneur's forte, to accomplish something excellent with as little resource as possible. Take for example a local fast food chain owner who did not know he was actually taking on the giants. He knew that these big corporation fast food chains spend time and a lot of money to do their market research before putting up a new branch. So this fledgling store owner simply built where the big stores are. His store will either be right across the street or on the other corner of the block. It worked! And now his company is worth twenty times more than when he started just a few years back.

TIP #26: THEY CREATE THE MARKET BY CREATING A NEED.

People do not know that they need something until they see it and it's available.

Tip #27: They do not spread themselves too thin.

There is a trick to this habit – the ability to say no. Experience will teach you that it's not a bad thing to decline to do a request once in a while. There will be people who would invest their time and knowledge in you and some of them would assume that they can cash in anytime. This dilemma goes with the territory, but you will find that there are people who would respect you more when they know you are not a doormat. Just remember that you became an entrepreneur because you want to be your own boss, so don't let others push you to the limits (that privilege is yours alone).

On the other hand, you will also find yourself wanting to do everything. You love to challenge yourself and in the process you may become overconfident. Learn to manage your schedule well, know your limitation and learn to delegate properly.

Tip #28: Invest on things that grow more and more valuable in time.

No one can blame us if we indulge in a little self-gratification especially after the completion of a big project. However, we should be careful about anything that depreciates as soon as you purchase it, unless absolutely necessary. Remember that (in general – antiques/vintages are excluded) cars, structures, gadgets, clothes (everything manufactured under the law of obsolescence) are included in this list. Do invest on a good vacation, because your rejuvenation is important to your well-being.

When you are simply looking for a place to invest your hard earned cash, do buy stocks and learn from Warren Buffet's principles: Rule #1 Never Lose Money; Rule#2 Never forget Rule #1.

www.ingramcontent.com/pod-product-compliance
Lightning Source LLC
Chambersburg PA
CBHW071818170526
45167CB00003B/1353